AF601844

the Big Book of
Bible
Promises

Written by Devin and Christen Kubricht
Scriptures selected by Devin and Christen Kubricht
Cover and design by Christen Kubricht
Copy Edited by Jonathan Sparks

ISBN: 979-8-218-23217-7

DEDICATION

This book is dedicated to Lily and Paige. Mom and Dad love you! No matter what you face in life, with Jesus you will always be victorious. We pray that you carry your 5 stones and sling, *The Word of God*, into every battle you face. If you do, you are sure to come out victorious!

Table of Contents

"God's word is alive and working. It is sharper than a sword sharpened on both sides. It cuts all the way into us, where the soul and the spirit are joined." Hebrews 4:12 ICB

Just as David faced the giant Goliath, you will face many giants in this life. Their names are fear, temptation, pride, loneliness, and many others. But like David, you have a weapon against the giants of life - The Living Word of God! We invite you to hunt for the treasure hidden in your very own Bible! This book is a tool in your hand to help you find Scripture verses you need when challenging moments arise. This book is meant to be a companion to your Bible and it is our hope that in reading this book it will cause you to further explore God's Word!

ANGER

Anger can often cause us to get in trouble. Moses got in trouble for his anger once. The people of Israel were arguing about not having water while they wandered in desert. God told Moses to speak to a rock and water would come out. But the people were shouting, grumbling and complaining. Moses got so mad at the people that he disobeyed God.

You see, in other times, Moses struck the rock with his staff and water came out (true story!!). But God wanted to test Moses' heart by telling him to ***speak*** to the rock instead.

Moses lost his cool and smacked the rock with his staff. Even though he was disobedient and angry, God caused the water to flow out so the people could drink. Sadly, Moses got angry, and did not obey God in that moment. Because of his actions, Moses could not enter the Promised Land.

It's easy to get angry. What we choose to do with that anger makes all the difference. We ***can*** be angry and not sin. We can also choose to let go of that anger. But most of all, if we do mess up…we can repent (change our minds), come back to Jesus and try again. After all, His mercies are new every morning!

"Stop being angry! Turn from your rage! Do not lose your temper— it only leads to harm." Psalm 37:8

"The LORD is merciful and compassionate, slow to get angry and filled with unfailing love." Psalm 145:8

"Short-tempered people do foolish things, and schemers are hated." Proverbs 14:17

"A gentle answer deflects anger, but harsh words make tempers flare." Proverbs 15:1

"A hot-tempered person starts fights; a cool-tempered person stops them." Proverbs 15:18

"Better to be patient than powerful; better to have self-control than to conquer a city." Proverbs 16:32

"Sensible people control their temper; they earn respect by overlooking wrongs." Proverbs 19:11

"If your enemies are hungry, give them food to eat. If they are thirsty, give them water to drink." Proverbs 25:21

"Dear friends, never take revenge. Leave that to the righteous anger of God. For the Scriptures say, 'I will take revenge; I will pay them back,' says the LORD."
Romans 12:19

"Don't sin by letting anger control you. Don't let the sun go down while you are still angry, for anger gives a foothold to the devil." Ephesians 4:26-27

"Get rid of all bitterness, rage, anger, harsh words, and slander, as well as all types of evil behavior. Instead, be kind to each other, tenderhearted, forgiving one another, just as God through Christ has forgiven you."
Ephesians 4:31-32

"Understand this, my dear brothers and sisters: You must all be quick to listen, slow to speak, and slow to get angry. Human anger does not produce the righteousness God desires." James 1:19-20

Is it ok to be angry?

____

____

What does the Bible say about being angry?

____

____

How can you use Bible Promises to help when you are angry?

____

____

God told Abram to leave his home country and go to a new land He promised to give to Abram and his children. Abram ***believed*** God! So, at 75 years old, he packed up and followed God to a far away country.

Abram did not have any children. On the journey, God promised Abram that he would have a son. What's more...he would have as many descendants as there are stars in the sky! Abram ***believed*** God!

One day, God made a covenant with Abram. He changed Abram's name to Abraham which means "Father of Many Nations". Finally, after believing God many years Abraham and his wife Sarah had a son, Isaac. From Abraham came the nation of Israel and eventually the Messiah - Jesus Christ! God did incredible things because Abraham ***believed*** God!

"Anything is possible if a person believes." Mark 9:23

"But to all who believed him and accepted him, He gave the right to become children of God." John 1:12

"For this is how God loved the world: He gave his one and only Son, so that everyone who believes in him will not perish but have eternal life." John 3:16

"And anyone who believes in God's Son has eternal life. Anyone who doesn't obey the Son will never experience eternal life but remains under God's angry judgment."John 3:36

"Jesus replied, 'I am the bread of life. Whoever comes to me will never be hungry again. Whoever believes in me will never be thirsty.'" John 6:35

"I tell you the truth, anyone who believes has eternal life." John 6:47

"I have come as a light to shine in this dark world, so that all who put their trust in me will no longer remain in the dark." John 12:46

"Then Jesus told him, 'You believe because you have seen me. Blessed are those who believe without seeing me.'"John 20:29

He is the one all the prophets testified about, saying that everyone who believes in him will have their sins forgiven through His name." Acts 10:43

What does it mean to believe God?

What can help us believe God?

Share about a time God spoke to you.

Word Search

T O D K J J J Y M A
R I M G T E H S Y B
U I B I O D S H F R
S O W E R D Y U P A
T D O N L A X P S H
R O M B T I C Z Q A
E U I C E H E L A M
L B A V A Y M V E G
Y T T R U S T S E G
M U E T O X J N Q X

believe	miracle	Abraham	trust
Jesus	doubt	obey	GOD
trust	rely		

Courage

Courage isn't the absence of fear, but rather trusting God even when we are scared. We all face scary things. A new school, a hard test, bullies, or the crazy neighborhood cat! Courage is holding on to Jesus when we are afraid because He will see us through!

Joshua was called to lead the People of Israel to conquer the Promised Land. He had to lead 3 million people into a new land to fight people that were bigger and stronger! (There were even giants in the land!) Even though he was a mighty warrior, Joshua was shaking in his boots! God reminded him to be strong and courageous. Joshua went on to lead the nation of Israel into the Promised Land. He couldn't have done it without Godly courage!

No matter what you are facing in life, you can trust Jesus to carry you through. He will give you the courage you need to do the right thing or face your fears!

"This is my command—be strong and courageous! Do not be afraid or discouraged. For the LORD your God is with you wherever you go." Joshua 1:9

"Don't be afraid!" Elisha told him. "For there are more on our side than on theirs!" Then Elisha prayed, "O LORD, open his eyes and let him see!" The LORD opened the young man's eyes, and when he looked up, he saw that the hillside around Elisha was filled with horses and chariots of fire." 2 Kings 6:16-17

"For he will conceal me there when troubles come; He will hide me in His sanctuary. He will place me out of reach on a high rock." Psalm 27:5

"Wait patiently for the LORD. Be brave and courageous. Yes, wait patiently for the LORD." Psalm 27:14

"Love the LORD, all you godly ones! For the LORD protects those who are loyal to him, but he harshly punishes the arrogant. So be strong and courageous, all you who put your hope in the LORD!" Psalm 31:23-24

"The LORD is the everlasting God, the Creator of all the earth. He never grows weak or weary. No one can measure the depths of his understanding. He gives power to the weak and strength to the powerless. Even youths will become weak and tired, and young men will fall in exhaustion. But those who trust in the LORD will find new strength. They will soar high on wings like eagles. They will run and not grow weary. They will walk and not faint."
Isaiah 40:28-31

"Do not be afraid, for I have ransomed you. I have called you by name; you are mine. When you go through deep waters, I will be with you. When you go through rivers of difficulty, you will not drown. When you walk through the fire of oppression, you will not be burned up; the flames will not consume you." Isaiah 43:1-2

"And now, O Lord, hear their threats, and give us, your servants, great boldness in preaching your word. Stretch out your hand with healing power; may miraculous signs and wonders be done through the name of your holy servant Jesus." After this prayer, the meeting place shook, and they were all filled with the Holy Spirit. Then they preached the word of God with boldness." Acts 4:29-31

What does courage mean to you?

____

____

How do you get the courage to do what is Godly?

____

____

What is your favorite Scripture about courage?

____

____

Enemies

In the movies, there's always a good guy and a bad guy. The hero always fights until he/she wins against the villain. Jesus had a different approach to defeating enemies. He called us to ***love our enemies***.

Jesus had a lot of friends, however because of His teachings, He made a lot of enemies with the religious rulers of the day. Jesus' enemies wanted to kill Him. These enemies had Jesus nailed to the cross. While Jesus hung on the cross he prayed **"Father, forgive them, for they don't know what they are doing." (Luke 23:34)**

His enemies were shouting mean things to Him and making fun of Him, and yet He prayed for them! Jesus showed us how to love our enemies that day.

God promises to help you when you face enemies. If you have an enemy, don't get even. Instead show them kindness and pray for that person!

Pray like this: Father, help me forgive my enemy. I pray that you bless them and help me to love them the way you do. In Jesus name, amen.

"For the LORD your God is going with you! He will fight for you against your enemies, and he will give you victory!" Deuteronomy 20:4

"The LORD will conquer your enemies when they attack you. They will attack you from one direction, but they will scatter from you in seven!" Deuteronomy 28:7

"Don't be afraid!" Elisha told him. "For there are more on our side than on theirs!" 2 Kings 6:16

"You must worship only the LORD your God. He is the one who will rescue you from all your enemies." 2 Kings 17:39

"The LORD is my light and my salvation— so why should I be afraid? The LORD is my fortress, protecting me from danger, so why should I tremble? When evil people come to devour me, when my enemies and foes attack me, they will stumble and fall. Though a mighty army surrounds me, my heart will not be afraid. Even if I am attacked, I will remain confident." Psalm 27:1-3

"The LORD rescues the Godly; he is their fortress in times of trouble. The LORD helps them, rescuing them from the wicked. He saves them, and they find shelter in him." Psalm 37:39-40

"You who love the LORD, hate evil! He protects the lives of his godly people and rescues them from the power of the wicked." Psalm 97:10

"When people's lives please the LORD, even their enemies are at peace with them." Proverbs 16:7

"You have heard the law that says, 'Love your neighbor' and hate your enemy. But I say, love your enemies! Pray for those who persecute you!" Matthew 5:43-44

"Dear friends, never take revenge. Leave that to the righteous anger of God. For the Scriptures say, "I will take revenge; I will pay them back," says the LORD. If your enemies are hungry, feed them. If they are thirsty, give them something to drink." Romans 12:19-20a

"So we can say with confidence, "The LORD is my helper, so I will have no fear. What can mere people do to me?" Hebrews 13:6

What does the Bible say we should do for our enemies?

____

____

What is your favorite Scripture about loving your enemies?

____

____

Share about a time Jesus helped you with a bully or enemy.

____

____

____

____

____

____

Envy is when we want something someone else has. Basically, we're not satisfied with what God has given us.

The writer of the book Ecclesiastes calls envy "chasing the wind". When we want things other people have, it's like we're chasing a blowing breeze. We reach for it and turn up with nothing!

In Luke, Jesus tells us not worry about what we will eat or the clothes we will wear because our Father in Heaven knows what we need and will provide it! Trust God with your needs and your wants!

"Don't worry about the wicked or envy those who do wrong." Psalm 37:1

"Don't envy violent people or copy their ways." Proverbs 3:31

"A peaceful heart leads to a healthy body; jealousy is like cancer in the bones." Proverbs 14:30

"Don't envy sinners, but always continue to fear the LORD. You will be rewarded for this; your hope will not be disappointed." Proverbs 23:17-18

"Don't envy evil people or desire their company. For their hearts plot violence, and their words always stir up trouble." Proverbs 24:1-2

"Anger is cruel, and wrath is like a flood, but jealousy is even more dangerous." Proverbs 27:4

"Then I observed that most people are motivated to success because they envy their neighbors. But this, too, is meaningless—like chasing the wind." Ecclesiastes 4:4

"And don't be concerned about what to eat and what to drink. Don't worry about such things. These things dominate the thoughts of unbelievers all over the world, but your Father already knows your needs. Seek the Kingdom of God above all else, and he will give you everything you need." Luke 12:29-31

"Those who belong to Christ Jesus have nailed the passions and desires of their sinful nature to his cross and crucified them there. Since we are living by the Spirit, let us follow the Spirit's leading in every part of our lives. Let us not become conceited, or provoke one another, or be jealous of one another." Galatians 5:24-26

"Jealousy and selfishness are not God's kind of wisdom. Such things are earthly, unspiritual, and demonic. For wherever there is jealousy and selfish ambition, there you will find disorder and evil of every kind." James 3:15-16

"You are jealous of what others have, but you can't get it, so you fight and wage war to take it away from them. Yet you don't have what you want because you don't ask God for it." James 4:2

Why is it bad to be envious?

What Scripture helps you when you feel envious?

Share about a time you were jealous of someone.

Eternal Life

You were created to live forever. When your body dies, your soul lives on. There are many stories and religious ideas about eternal life, but the Word of God explains the truth about life after death.

Once your body dies, you leave the earth and journey to Eternity. **Eternity means forever**. People who believe in Jesus and live for Him, will be welcomed into Heaven, a place of beauty and life where God himself dwells. People who don't believe in God or turn their hearts away from Him will be sent to Hell, a place of Eternal punishment, darkness, and pain.

Heaven and Hell are very real. We all are born into sin (separation from God) because Adam and Eve sinned by disobeying God. Jesus made a way for us to escape Hell by offering Himself as a sacrifice for our sins. When we trust in Jesus and live for God, the way to Heaven is open to us.

When you are with Jesus, eternity isn't scary. In fact, you will be ruling and reigning with Him in eternity as sons and daughters. When we come to Jesus as our Savior, we will be kings and queens with Jesus forever! It's important to tell everyone you know about Jesus so they can be welcomed into heaven too!

"But as for me, I know that my Redeemer lives, and he will stand upon the earth at last. And after my body has decayed, yet in my body I will see God! I will see Him for myself. Yes, I will see him with my own eyes. I am overwhelmed at the thought!" Job 19:25-27

"But those who die in the LORD will live; their bodies will rise again! Those who sleep in the earth will rise up and sing for joy!" Isaiah 26:19a

"For this is how God loved the world: He gave his one and only Son, so that everyone who believes in him will not perish but have eternal life." John 3:16

"Don't be so surprised! Indeed, the time is coming when all the dead in their graves will hear the voice of God's Son, and they will rise again. Those who have done good will rise to experience eternal life, and those who have continued in evil will rise to experience judgment." John 5:28-29

"I tell you the truth, anyone who believes has eternal life." John 6:47

"I am the resurrection and the life. Anyone who believes in me will live, even after dying. Everyone who lives in me and believes in me will never ever die." John 11:25-26

"Don't let your hearts be troubled. Trust in God, and trust also in me. There is more than enough room in my Father's home. If this were not so, would I have told you that I am going to prepare a place for you? When everything is ready, I will come and get you, so that you will always be with Me where I am. And you know the way to where I am going." John 14:1-4

"For the wages of sin is death, but the free gift of God is eternal life through Christ Jesus our Lord." Romans 6:23

"But there is an order to this resurrection: Christ was raised as the first of the harvest; then all who belong to Christ will be raised when he comes back." 1 Corinthians 15:23

"Our bodies are buried in brokenness, but they will be raised in glory. They are buried in weakness, but they will be raised in strength. They are buried as natural human bodies, but they will be raised as spiritual bodies. For just as there are natural bodies, there are also spiritual bodies." 1 Corinthians 15:43-44

"But let me reveal to you a wonderful secret. We will not all die, but we will all be transformed! It will happen in a moment, in the blink of an eye, when the last trumpet is blown. For when the trumpet sounds, those who have died will be raised to live forever. And we who are living will also be transformed."1 Corinthians 15:51-52

"Death is swallowed up in victory. O death, where is your victory? O death, where is your sting?" 1 Corinthians 15:54-55

"Those who live only to satisfy their own sinful nature will harvest decay and death from that sinful nature. But those who live to please the Spirit will harvest everlasting life from the Spirit." Galatians 6:8

What does Eternal Life mean?

How can you spend Eternity with Jesus?

How can we use these Scriptures to help us?

A lot of people talk about faith. But what is faith really? Faith is simply believing God even when we can't see a way.

One day, the disciples were in a boat during a terrible storm. The wind was blowing and it was raining. The waves were making the boat dip up and down. Suddenly they saw Jesus walking ON the storm tossed Sea of Galilee like it was dry ground!

Peter saw this and said, "Tell me to come out on the water!" And Jesus said, "Yes, come!" Through the rain, and howling wind he stepped out into the water!

The only way this was possible was because Peter had faith. Do you need a miracle? Jesus tells us to ask in faith! Watch and see God move!

"Keep on asking, and you will receive what you ask for. Keep on seeking, and you will find. Keep on knocking, and the door will be opened to you." Matthew 7:7

Then Jesus told them, "I tell you the truth, if you have faith and don't doubt, you can do things like this and much more. You can even say to this mountain, 'May you be lifted up and thrown into the sea,' and it will happen. You can pray for anything, and if you have faith, you will receive it." Matthew 21:21-22

"Through faith in the name of Jesus, this man was healed—and you know how crippled he was before. Faith in Jesus' name has healed him before your very eyes." Acts 3:16

"So faith comes from hearing, that is, hearing the Good News about Christ." Romans 10:17

"For we live by believing and not by seeing." 2 Corinthians 5:7

"For you are all children of God through faith in Christ Jesus. And all who have been united with Christ in baptism have put on Christ, like putting on new clothes." Galatians 3:26-27

"God saved you by his grace when you believed. And you can't take credit for this; it is a gift from God."
Ephesians 2:8

"Then Christ will make his home in your hearts as you trust in him. Your roots will grow down into God's love and keep you strong. And may you have the power to understand, as all God's people should, how wide, how long, how high, and how deep his love is."
Ephesians 3:17-18

"Faith shows the reality of what we hope for; it is the evidence of things we cannot see." Hebrews 11:1

"And it is impossible to please God without faith. Anyone who wants to come to him must believe that God exists and that he rewards those who sincerely seek him."
Hebrews 11:6

What is faith?

____

____

What Scripture explains faith?

____

Does Jesus see our faith? How?

____

____

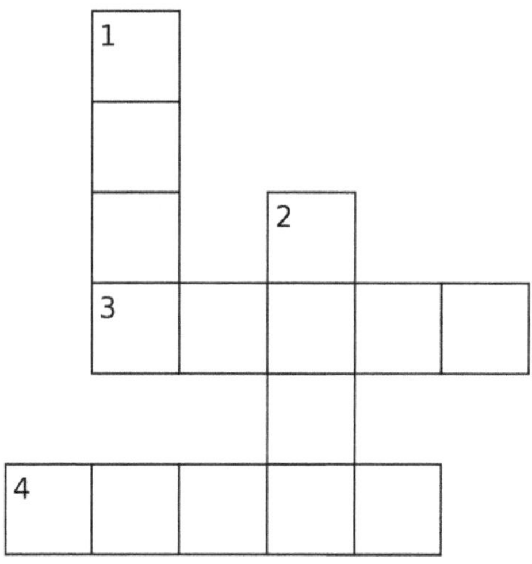

Down:

1. Your vision spheres
2. A vessel for a river, lake or ocean

Across:

3. Rain, wind and lightning
4. The reality of what we hope for; it is the evidence of things we cannot see

Answer key:
1. eyes 3. storm
2. boat 4. faith

The Bible says "Don't be afraid" and "Fear not" a total of 365 times! God's word offers a daily reminder to not be afraid!

But let's face it. We all get scared sometimes! Whether you're afraid of the dark, scared of spiders or afraid to speak in front of a crowd - fear is real! But with God we can overcome our fears!

Gideon was a man that lived in Bible times and he was a scaredy cat! At that time, the Nation of Israel were being bullied by the Midianites because they had been disobedient to God. The bullies would come and steal all the people's food so they had nothing to eat! Gideon was afraid so he hid while he was threshing wheat so his food wouldn't be stolen. An Angel came and called Gideon a "Mighty Man of God"! But Gideon did not feel so mighty. He was scared! With God's help, Gideon became a mighty warrior and led 300 men to fight against the bully Midianites.

Jesus knows when you are scared, and He is with you every moment. He doesn't call you a scaredy cat... He calls you ***MIGHTY!***

"This is my command— Be strong and courageous! Do not be afraid or discouraged. For the LORD your God is with you wherever you go." Joshua 1:9

"Even when I walk through the darkest valley, I will not be afraid, for you are close beside me. Your rod and your staff protect and comfort me." Psalm 23:4

"The LORD is my light and my salvation—so why should I be afraid? The LORD is my fortress, protecting me from danger, so why should I tremble? When evil people come to devour me, when my enemies and foes attack me, they will stumble and fall. Though a mighty army surrounds me, my heart will not be afraid. Even if I am attacked, I will remain confident." Psalm 27:1-3

"I prayed to the LORD, and he answered me. He freed me from all my fears." Psalm 34:4

"God is our refuge and strength, always ready to help in times of trouble." Psalm 46:1

"He will cover you with his feathers. He will shelter you with his wings. His faithful promises are your armor and protection. Do not be afraid of the terrors of the night, nor the arrow that flies in the day. Do not dread the disease that stalks in darkness, nor the disaster that strikes at midday." Psalm 91:4-6

"The LORD is for me, so I will have no fear. What can mere people do to me?" Psalm 118:6

"You can go to bed without fear; you will lie down and sleep soundly. You need not be afraid of sudden disaster or the destruction that comes upon the wicked, for the LORD is your security. He will keep your foot from being caught in a trap." Proverbs 3:24-26

"Fearing people is a dangerous trap, but trusting the LORD means safety." Proverbs 29:25

"For I hold you by your right hand, the LORD your God. And I say to you, 'Don't be afraid. I am here to help you... don't be afraid, people of Israel, for I will help you. I am the LORD, your Redeemer. I am the Holy One of Israel." Isaiah 41:13-14b

"Do not be afraid, for I have ransomed you. I have called you by name; you are Mine. When you go through deep waters, I will be with you. When you go through rivers of difficulty, you will not drown. When you walk through the fire of oppression, you will not be burned up; the flames will not consume you." Isaiah 43:1-2

"Seek the Kingdom of God above all else, and he will give you everything you need. "So don't be afraid, little flock. For it gives your Father great happiness to give you the Kingdom." Luke 12:31-32

"I am leaving you with a gift—peace of mind and heart. And the peace I give is a gift the world cannot give. So don't be troubled or afraid." John 14:27

"You have not received a spirit that makes you fearful slaves. Instead, you received God's Spirit when He adopted you as His own children. Now we call him, "Abba, Father." For His Spirit joins with our spirit to affirm that we are God's children." Romans 8:15-16

"For God has not given us a spirit of fear and timidity, but of power, love, and self-discipline." 2 Timothy 1:7

"Give all your worries and cares to God, for He cares about you." 1 Peter 5:7

Is it ok to be afraid? Why or why not?

____

____

How does Jesus help us when we are afraid?

____

____

Share a time Jesus helped you when you were scared.

____

____

Word Scramble

EFRA ____________

UAREOGC ____________

RKDA ____________

GITLH ____________

SRIPDE ____________

URSTT ____________

ESUSJ ____________

PLEH ____________

ERGDAN ____________

EAFS ____________

Answer key:
Fear, courage, dark, light, spider, trust, Jesus, help, danger, safe

Forgiveness

One Day a king decided to see who owed him money. One guy was brought in who owed the king millions of dollars! He couldn't pay, so his master ordered that he go to jail to pay the debt. But the man begged him, "Please, be patient with me, and I will pay it all." The master was filled with pity, and he released him and forgave his debt!

Later, the forgiven man went to a fellow servant who owed him a few thousand dollars. He grabbed him by the throat saying "Pay me what you owe now!" His fellow servant begged for a little more time. "Please be patient with me, and I will pay it!" He said. But the man wouldn't wait. He had the man arrested and put in prison!

Some of the other servants saw this, and were very upset. They went to the king and told him everything. The king called in the man he had forgiven and said, "You evil servant! I forgave you a huge debt because you begged me. ***Shouldn't you have mercy on your fellow servant, just as I had mercy on you?***" Then the angry king sent the man to prison.

Jesus wants you to forgive people who wrong you. But if you refuse, you will be like the man who was forgiven a multi-million dollar debt, yet wouldn't forgive a few thousand dollars. We cannot enter heaven with un-forgiveness in our hearts. If someone wrongs you, pray and ask Jesus to help you forgive them!

"If your enemies are hungry, give them food to eat. If they are thirsty, give them water to drink." Proverbs 25:21

"Love your enemies! Pray for those who persecute you! In that way, you will be acting as true children of your Father in heaven. " Matthew 5:44

"If you forgive those who sin against you, your heavenly Father will forgive you. But if you refuse to forgive others, your Father will not forgive your sins." Matthew 6:14-15

"But when you are praying, first forgive anyone you are holding a grudge against, so that your Father in heaven will forgive your sins, too." Mark 11:25

"Do not judge others, and you will not be judged. Do not condemn others, or it will all come back against you. Forgive others, and you will be forgiven. Give, and you will receive. Your gift will return to you in full—pressed down, shaken together to make room for more, running over, and poured into your lap. The amount you give will determine the amount you get back." Luke 6:37-38

"Get rid of all bitterness, rage, anger, harsh words, and slander, as well as all types of evil behavior. Instead, be kind to each other, tenderhearted, forgiving one another, just as God through Christ has forgiven you."
Ephesians 4:31-32

"But if we confess our sins to Him, He is faithful and just to forgive us our sins and to cleanse us from all wickedness."
1 John 1:9

What does it mean to forgive someone?

Should we forgive others? Why?

Share about a time when you had to forgive someone.

GOD's Love

Did you know that God loves you? We're not talking about regular love. This love is as deep as the ocean, as high as the tallest mountain and as precious as the rarest diamond.

God's love is bigger than the whole universe! The Bible says that our amazing God loves you and thinks about you. And what's more, Jesus died to save you from your sins so you can be with Him for all eternity!

You were created to have a relationship with God. He wants you to love Him. Spend time each day talking to God and thanking Him for His unfailing love!

"Our faithful God keeps His promises for a thousand generations and lavishes his unfailing love on those who love him and obey his commands." Deuteronomy 7:9

"Your unfailing love, O LORD, is as vast as the heavens; your faithfulness reaches beyond the clouds. Your righteousness is like the mighty mountains, your justice like the ocean depths. You care for people and animals alike, O LORD. How precious is your unfailing love, O God! All humanity finds shelter in the shadow of your wings" Psalm 36:5-7

"But you, O Lord, are a God of compassion and mercy, slow to get angry and filled with unfailing love and faithfulness." Psalm 86:15

"Help me, O LORD my God! Save me because of your unfailing love." Psalm 109:26

How precious are your thoughts about me, O God. They cannot be numbered! I can't even count them; they outnumber the grains of sand!" Psalms 139:17-18

"'For the mountains may move and the hills disappear, but even then my faithful love for you will remain. My covenant of blessing will never be broken,' says the LORD, who has mercy on you." Isaiah 54:10

"'For the mountains may move and the hills disappear, but even then My faithful love for you will remain. My covenant of blessing will never be broken,' says the LORD, who has mercy on you." Isaiah 54:10

"Long ago the LORD said to Israel: 'I have loved you, my people, with an everlasting love. With unfailing love I have drawn you to Myself.'" Jeremiah 31:3

"The LORD says, 'Then I will heal you of your faithlessness; my love will know no bounds, for my anger will be gone forever.'" Hosea 14:4

"The LORD your God is living among you. He is a mighty savior. He will take delight in you with gladness. With His love, He will calm all your fears. He will rejoice over you with joyful songs." Zephaniah 3:17

"For this is how God loved the world: He gave His one and only Son, so that everyone who believes in Him will not perish but have eternal life." John 3:16

"There is no greater love than to lay down one's life for one's friends." John 15:13

"Neither death nor life, neither angels nor demons, neither our fears for today nor our worries about tomorrow—not even the powers of hell can separate us from God's love. No power in the sky above or in the earth below—indeed, nothing in all creation will ever be able to separate us from the love of God that is revealed in Christ Jesus our Lord." Romans 8:38-39

"Christ will make his home in your hearts as you trust in Him. Your roots will grow down into God's love and keep you strong. And may you have the power to understand, as all God's people should, how wide, how long, how high, and how deep His love is." Ephesians 3:17-18

"Now may our Lord Jesus Christ himself and God our Father, who loved us and by His grace gave us eternal comfort and a wonderful hope, comfort you and strengthen you in every good thing you do and say." 2 Thessalonians 2:16-17

"God showed how much He loved us by sending His one and only Son into the world so that we might have eternal life through Him. This is real love—not that we loved God, but that He loved us and sent His Son as a sacrifice to take away our sins." 1 John 4:9-10

How do you know Jesus loves you?

How should you respond to the love of Jesus?

Share about a time when you felt God's love.

Word Search

Z	F	L	J	E	S	U	S	K	I
J	F	R	I	D	N	P	U	O	M
K	L	F	R	I	E	N	D	Y	E
F	E	T	E	R	N	I	T	Y	R
R	B	M	A	A	X	K	A	E	C
E	T	X	L	Y	N	V	H	X	Y
E	F	A	I	T	H	F	U	L	L
D	F	X	C	Y	Q	J	M	G	O
O	P	H	O	P	E	B	X	O	V
M	A	Z	O	S	F	K	V	D	E

Faithful
Friend
Jesus
Freedom
Mercy
Love
Eternity
Hope
GOD

Are you in trouble? God will come to your rescue! Ask Jesus for help when you are afraid, anxious, or in trouble.

Sometimes in life we feel all alone and overwhelmed by the problems that surround us like a flood. The Bible tells us that God is our Strong Tower, our Refuge, our Hiding Place, our Shield. Don't be afraid, He will protect you!

Pray like this: "God, I need help. Please protect me and deliver me. In Jesus name, amen!"

"But you, O Lord, are a shield around me; you are my glory, the one who holds my head high." Psalm 3:3

"For you bless the godly, O Lord; you surround them with your shield of love." Psalm 5:12

"The LORD is a shelter for the oppressed, a refuge in times of trouble. Those who know your name trust in you, for you, O LORD, do not abandon those who search for you." Psalm 9:9-10

"I love you, LORD; you are my strength. The LORD is my rock, my fortress, and my savior; my God is my rock, in whom I find protection. He is my shield, the power that saves me, and my place of safety. I called on the LORD, who is worthy of praise, and he saved me from my enemies." Psalm 18:1-3

"For he has not ignored or belittled the suffering of the needy. He has not turned his back on them, but has listened to their cries for help." Psalm 22:24

"Praise the LORD! For he has heard my cry for mercy. The LORD is my strength and shield. I trust him with all my heart. He helps me, and my heart is filled with joy. I burst out in songs of thanksgiving." Psalm 28:6-7

"The LORD protects those who are loyal to him, but he harshly punishes the arrogant. So be strong and courageous, all you who put your hope in the LORD!" Psalm 31:23-24

"For you are my hiding place; you protect me from trouble. You surround me with songs of victory." Psalm 32:7

"The LORD directs the steps of the godly. He delights in every detail of their lives. Though they stumble, they will never fall, for the LORD holds them by the hand." Psalm 37:23-24

"The LORD rescues the Godly; he is their fortress in times of trouble. The LORD helps them, rescuing them from the wicked. He saves them, and they find shelter in him." Psalm 37:39-40

"My health may fail, and my spirit may grow weak, but God remains the strength of my heart; He is mine forever." Psalm 73:26

"This I declare about the LORD: He alone is my refuge, my place of safety; He is my God, and I trust him." Psalm 91:2

"If you make the LORD your refuge, if you make the Most High your shelter, no evil will conquer you; no plague will come near your home. For he will order his angels to protect you wherever you go." Psalm 91:9-11

"The LORD says, 'I will rescue those who love me. I will protect those who trust in my name. When they call on me, I will answer; I will be with them in trouble. I will rescue and honor them.'" Psalm 91:14-15

"All you who fear the Lord, trust the Lord! He is your helper and your shield." Psalm 115:11

"Every word of God proves true. He is a shield to all who come to him for protection." Proverbs 30:5

"I will answer them before they even call to me. While they are still talking about their needs, I will go ahead and answer their prayers!" Isaiah 65:24

"I will not leave you as orphans; I will come to you."
John 14:18

How can you ask Jesus for help in times of trouble?

____

____

What is your favorite Scripture about help from God?

____

____

Share about a time when Jesus helped you.

____

____

____

Down:

1. A commitment
2. Lending a Hand
5. A safe place

Across:

3. Tough times
4. Someone who saves
6. To keep safe

Answer key:
1. promise 4. savior
2. help 5. refuge
3. trouble 6. protect

Healing 😲

God wants to heal us when we have sicknesses or injuries. The Bible talks about a man that was born blind who one day met Jesus.

The man asked Jesus to heal him and Jesus did something really weird... Jesus spat on the ground, made mud and rubbed it in the man's eyes! Then, he told him to go wash in the Pool of Siloam. He went and washed and when he opened his eyes... HE COULD SEE!!! For the first time in his life he saw the blue sky, white clouds, green trees, and the colorful kaleidoscope of people!

The Pharisees (the Religious Leaders) tried to discredit the miracle Jesus did. First, they asked the man's parents "Was your son really born blind or is he faking?!" The man's parents told them he really ***was*** blind! The Pharisees went to the man and tried to bully him to change his story. They told the formerly blind man that Jesus was a just sinner! (Not true!) The man said, "Whether he is a sinner or not, I don't know. ***One thing I do know. I was blind but now I see!"***

Jesus is still healing people today! The Bible says God is the same yesterday, today and forever! If you need healing, ask Jesus!

"Let all that I am praise the LORD; may I never forget the good things he does for me. He forgives all my sins and heals all my diseases." Psalm 103:2-3

"He heals the brokenhearted and bandages their wounds." Psalm 147:3

"Yet it was our weaknesses he carried; it was our sorrows that weighed him down. And we thought his troubles were a punishment from God, a punishment for his own sins! But he was pierced for our rebellion, crushed for our sins. He was beaten so we could be whole. He was whipped so we could be healed."
Isaiah 53:4-5

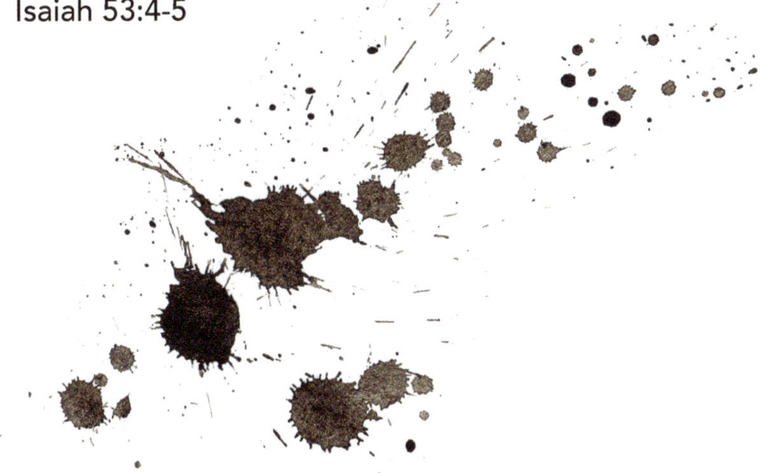

"The Spirit of the Sovereign LORD is upon me, for the LORD has anointed me to bring good news to the poor. He has sent me to comfort the brokenhearted and to proclaim that captives will be released and prisoners will be freed." Isaiah 61:1

"O LORD, if you heal me, I will be truly healed; if you save me, I will be truly saved. My praises are for you alone!" Jeremiah 17:14

"But for you who fear my name, the Sun of Righteousness will rise with healing in his wings. And you will go free, leaping with joy like calves let out to pasture." Malachi 4:2

"Suddenly, a man with leprosy approached him and knelt before him. "Lord," the man said, "if you are willing, you can heal me and make me clean." Jesus reached out and touched him. "I am willing," he said. "Be healed!" And instantly the leprosy disappeared." Matthew 8:2-3

"When Jesus saw him and knew he had been ill for a long time, he asked him, "Would you like to get well?" "I can't, sir," the sick man said, "for I have no one to put me into the pool when the water bubbles up. Someone else always gets there ahead of me." Jesus told him, "Stand up, pick up your mat, and walk!"Instantly, the man was healed! He rolled up his sleeping mat and began walking! But this miracle happened on the Sabbath." John 5:6-9

"Are any of you sick? You should call for the elders of the church to come and pray over you, anointing you with oil in the name of the Lord. Such a prayer offered in faith will heal the sick, and the Lord will make you well. And if you have committed any sins, you will be forgiven."
James 5:14-15

"He personally carried our sins in his body on the cross so that we can be dead to sin and live for what is right. By His wounds you are healed." 1 Peter 2:24

Does God still heal people today?

What is your favorite healing Scripture?

Do you need healing? Write out your prayer here.

Word Search

C	W	M	Y	Y	X	R	P	L	Q
E	S	F	W	C	T	X	E	S	G
K	D	A	A	G	A	Q	Y	L	I
U	K	E	V	I	H	M	E	I	H
E	B	G	L	E	T	E	S	F	H
A	O	V	P	I	C	H	A	E	O
R	A	Q	S	Y	V	T	L	L	P
S	Z	O	J	A	N	E	Z	H	E
O	L	P	P	T	B	H	R	V	E
U	F	S	C	B	F	R	F	G	C

Deliver	Faith	Heal	Save
Hope	Life	Eyes	Ears

Holy Spirit

The Holy Spirit is the Spirit or breath of God. Jesus speaks about the Holy Spirit in John 14. "I will ask the Father, and He will give you another Advocate, who will never leave you. He is the Holy Spirit, who leads you into all truth." John 14:16-17a

In Acts chapter 2, we see people being Baptized in the Holy Spirit. This means that they were so filled up with the Holy Spirit that they began speak in languages they did not know and speak about the greatness of God.

God wants to give you His Holy Spirit. Ask God for the gift of the Holy Spirit. Pray in faith, knowing that He wants to give this amazing gift! (Read Luke 11:11-13)

Pray like this: "God, I want to grow closer to you and be more like Jesus. Please baptize me in your Holy Spirit. In Jesus name, amen!"

"At that time the Spirit of the LORD will come powerfully upon you, and you will prophesy with them. You will be changed into a different person." 1 Samuel 10:6

"And this is my covenant with them," says the LORD. "My Spirit will not leave them, and neither will these words I have given you. They will be on your lips and on the lips of your children and your children's children forever. I, the LORD, have spoken!" Isaiah 59:21

"And I will give you a new heart, and I will put a new spirit in you. I will take out your stony, stubborn heart and give you a tender, responsive heart. And I will put my Spirit in you so that you will follow my decrees and be careful to obey my regulations." Ezekiel 36:26-27

"I baptize with water those who repent of their sins and turn to God. But someone is coming soon who is greater than I am—so much greater that I'm not worthy even to be his slave and carry his sandals. He will baptize you with the Holy Spirit and with fire." Matthew 3:11

"You fathers—if your children ask for a fish, do you give them a snake instead? Or if they ask for an egg, do you give them a scorpion? Of course not! So if you sinful people know how to give good gifts to your children, how much more will your heavenly Father give the Holy Spirit to those who ask him." Luke 11:11-13

Jesus replied, "Anyone who drinks this water will soon become thirsty again. But those who drink the water I give will never be thirsty again. It becomes a fresh, bubbling spring within them, giving them eternal life." John 4:13-14

"I will ask the Father, and He will give you another Advocate, who will never leave you. He is the Holy Spirit, who leads you into all truth." John 14:16-17a

I am telling you these things now while I am still with you. But when the Father sends the Advocate as my representative—that is, the Holy Spirit—he will teach you everything and will remind you of everything I have told you." John 14:25-26

When the Spirit of truth comes, He will guide you into all truth. He will not speak on His own but will tell you what He has heard. He will tell you about the future. He will bring me glory by telling you whatever He receives from me." John 16:13-14

"On the day of Pentecost all the believers were meeting together in one place. Suddenly, there was a sound from heaven like the roaring of a mighty windstorm, and it filled the house where they were sitting. Then, what looked like flames or tongues of fire appeared and settled on each of them. And everyone present was filled with the Holy Spirit and began speaking in other languages, as the Holy Spirit gave them this ability." Acts 2:1-4

"The Spirit of God, who raised Jesus from the dead, lives in you. And just as God raised Christ Jesus from the dead, He will give life to your mortal bodies by this same Spirit living within you." Romans 8:11

"And the Holy Spirit helps us in our weakness. For example, we don't know what God wants us to pray for. But the Holy Spirit prays for us with groanings that cannot be expressed in words. And the Father who knows all hearts knows what the Spirit is saying, for the Spirit pleads for us believers in harmony with God's own will." Romans 8:26-27

"And we have received God's Spirit (not the world's spirit), so we can know the wonderful things God has freely given us." 1 Corinthians 2:12

"Through Christ Jesus, God has blessed the Gentiles with the same blessing he promised to Abraham, so that we who are believers might receive the promised Holy Spirit through faith."Galatians 3:14

"Let the Holy Spirit guide your lives. Then you won't be doing what your sinful nature craves. The sinful nature wants to do evil, which is just the opposite of what the Spirit wants. And the Spirit gives us desires that are the opposite of what the sinful nature desires. These two forces are constantly fighting each other, so you are not free to carry out your good intentions." Galatians 5:16-17

What is the Baptism of the Holy Spirit?

____

____

How does the Holy Spirit help us?

____

____

What is your favorite Scripture about the Holy Spirit?

____

____

Honesty

Have you ever told a lie? Lies multiply like fleas on a dog's back! Once you tell one, you might have to tell another. Then another... until you can't remember what's true or false.

The Bible teaches us to tell the truth. Even one of the Ten Commandments says not to give false witness (lie). Have you ever wondered why? When we speak truth, we honor God and those around us. Jesus wants you to be honest and promises to bless you if you will deal honestly with others.

"You must not testify falsely against your neighbor." Exodus 20:16

"Who may climb the mountain of the LORD? Who may stand in his holy place? Only those whose hands and hearts are pure, who do not worship idols and never tell lies." Psalm 24:3-4

"He grants a treasure of common sense to the honest. He is a shield to those who walk with integrity." Proverbs 2:7

"Truthful words stand the test of time, but lies are soon exposed." Proverbs 12:19

"The LORD detests lying lips, but he delights in those who tell the truth." Proverbs 12:22

"An honest witness does not lie; a false witness breathes lies." Proverbs 14:5

"The LORD is more pleased when we do what is right and just than when we offer him sacrifices." Proverbs 21:3

"Instead, we will speak the truth in love, growing in every way more and more like Christ, who is the head of his body, the church." Ephesians 4:15

"So stop telling lies. Let us tell our neighbors the truth, for we are all parts of the same body." Ephesians 4:25

"Don't lie to each other, for you have stripped off your old sinful nature and all its wicked deeds. Put on your new nature, and be renewed as you learn to know your Creator and become like him." Colossians 3:9-10

Is being honest easy? Why or why not?

____

____

Why does Jesus want us to be honest?

____

____

What is your favorite Scripture about being honest?

____

____

Identity

Have you ever wondered "Who am I?" or "What will I be when I grow up?" The world around you will try to tell you who you should be. But God's Word will help you understand your ***true identity***.

God calls you His child. He has adopted you into His family. You are so precious to Him that He keeps track of the number of hairs on your head! He knew you before you were even born. He knitted you together in your Mother's womb. He chose your eye color, your hair color and your beautiful smile! Indeed, you are fearfully and wonderfully made!

You were created by God on purpose with a purpose. Each person's purpose is unique. Most importantly, you were created to live in relationship with Jesus Christ.

"So God created human beings in his own image. In the image of God he created them; male and female He created them." Genesis 1:27

"Then the LORD God formed the man from the dust of the ground. He breathed the breath of
life into the man's nostrils, and the man became a living person." Genesis 2:7

"You made all the delicate, inner parts of my body and knit me together in my mother's womb. Thank you for making me so wonderfully complex! Your workmanship is marvelous—how well I know it."
Psalm 139:13-14

"But now, O Jacob, listen to the LORD who created you. O Israel, the one who formed you says, "Do not be afraid, for I have ransomed you. I have called you by name; you are mine."Isaiah 43:1

"And yet, O LORD, you are our Father. We are the clay, and you are the potter. We all are formed by your hand."
Isaiah 64:8

"I knew you before I formed you in your mother's womb. Before you were born I set you apart and appointed you as my prophet to the nations." Jeremiah 1:5

"For I know the plans I have for you," says the LORD.
"They are plans for good and not for disaster,
to give you a future and a hope." Jeremiah 29:11

"But to all who believed him and accepted him, he gave the right to become children of God. They are reborn—not with a physical birth resulting from human passion or plan, but a birth that comes from God." John 1:12-13

"This means that anyone who belongs to Christ has become a new person. The old life is gone; a new life has begun!" 2 Corinthians 5:17

"My old self has been crucified with Christ. It is no longer I who live, but Christ lives in me. So I live in this earthly body by trusting in the Son of God, who loved me and gave himself for me." Galatians 2:20

"For you are all children of God through faith in Christ Jesus. And all who have been united with Christ in baptism have put on Christ, like putting on new clothes. There is no longer Jew or Gentile, slave or free, male and female. For you are all one in Christ Jesus. And now that you belong to Christ, you are the true children of Abraham. You are his heirs, and God's promise to Abraham belongs to you." Galatians 3:26-29

"For we are God's masterpiece. He has created us anew in Christ Jesus, so we can do the good things he planned for us long ago." Ephesians 2:10

"Put on your new nature, created to be like God—truly righteous and holy." Ephesians 4:24

"You are a chosen people. You are royal priests, a holy nation, God's very own possession. As a result, you can show others the goodness of God, for he called you out of the darkness into his wonderful light." 1 Peter 2:9

What is unique about you?

What does it mean to be a Child of God?

God created you for a purpose. What do you want to be when you grow up?

Word Scramble

MI	__________
UENUIQ	__________
DGO	__________
ETCDEAR	__________
EM	__________
NO	__________
PUPOSER	__________
ORF	__________
ISH	__________
EPSRPUO	__________

Answer key:
I'm unique. God created me on purpose for His purpose!

Loneliness

Have you ever felt alone? Like you don't fit in or belong? We all feel alone sometimes. The fear of loneliness can change the way we behave, and lead us do things we shouldn't do because we don't want to be alone.

God says you are ***never alone***. Jesus is with you always. He knows that you need friends and family. Psalms 68:6 says, "God places the lonely in families" God will connect you with people who love you and want to help you grow.

God wants you to be a part of a church family. It is important to meet together in Church with our Spiritual Family so we can grow.

If you feel alone, Jesus is always there with you. He will comfort you, help you, and stay right beside you no matter what. Jesus is the friend tha sticks closer than a brother!

"So be strong and courageous! Do not be afraid and do not panic before them. For the Lord your God will personally go ahead of you. He will neither fail you nor abandon you." Deuteronomy 31:6

"The Lord will not abandon his people, because that would dishonor his great name. For it has pleased the Lord to make you his very own people." 1 Samuel 12:22

"Father to the fatherless, defender of widows— this is God, whose dwelling is holy. God places the lonely in families; he sets the prisoners free and gives them joy." Psalms 68:5-6

"I can never escape from your Spirit! I can never get away from your presence! If I go up to heaven, you are there; if I go down to the grave, you are there. If I ride the wings of the morning, if I dwell by the farthest oceans, even there your hand will guide me, and your strength will support me." Psalms 139:7-10

"I have called you back from the ends of the earth, saying, 'You are my servant.' For I have chosen you and will not throw you away. Don't be afraid, for I am with you. Don't be discouraged, for I am your God. I will strengthen you and help you. I will hold you up with my victorious right hand." Isaiah 41:9-10

"I am with you always, even to the end of the age." Matthew 28:20

"Neither death nor life, neither angels nor demons, neither our fears for today nor our worries about tomorrow—not even the powers of hell can separate us from God's love. No power in the sky above or in the earth below—indeed, nothing in all creation will ever be able to separate us from the love of God that is revealed in Christ Jesus our Lord." Romans 8:38-39

"And God has given us his Spirit as proof that we live in Him and He in us." 1 John 4:13

What can you do when you feel alone?

Who is there with you no matter what?

Share about a time when you felt alone.

Obedience

Obeying the rules can be hard. Sometimes we want to have fun when parents tell us it's time to do chores or eat dinner. Obeying your parents is important because they protect you and guide you.

Obeying God is ***even more*** important because when we obey Him, we are in His will - protected and blessed.

James said it best when he wrote, "Don't just listen to God's word. You must ***do*** what it says. Otherwise, you are only fooling yourselves. For if you listen to the word and don't obey, it is like glancing at your face in a mirror. You see yourself, walk away, and forget what you look like. But if you look carefully into the perfect law that sets you free, and if you do what it says and don't forget what you heard, then God will bless you for doing it." (James 1:22-25)

"The LORD your God will delight in you if you obey his voice and keep the commands and decrees written in this Book of Instruction, and if you turn to the LORD your God with all your heart and soul."
Deuteronomy 30:10

But Samuel replied, "What is more pleasing to the LORD: your burnt offerings and sacrifices or your obedience to His voice? Listen! Obedience is better than sacrifice, and submission is better than offering the fat of rams." 1 Samuel 15:22

"So if you ignore the least commandment and teach others to do the same, you will be called the least in the Kingdom of Heaven. But anyone who obeys God's laws and teaches them will be called great in the Kingdom of Heaven." Matthew 5:19

"Not everyone who calls out to me, 'Lord! Lord!' will enter the Kingdom of Heaven. Only those who actually do the will of my Father in heaven will enter." Matthew 7:21

"Anyone who listens to my teaching and follows it is wise, like a person who builds a house on solid rock. Though the rain comes in torrents and the floodwaters rise and the winds beat against that house, it won't collapse because it is built on bedrock. But anyone who hears my teaching and doesn't obey it is foolish, like a person who builds a house on sand. When the rains and floods come and the winds beat against that house, it will collapse with a mighty crash." Matthew 7:24-27

Jesus replied, "But even more blessed are all who hear the word of God and put it into practice." Luke 11:28

"All who love me will do what I say. My Father will love them, and we will come and make our home with each of them." John 14:23

"When you obey my commandments, you remain in my love, just as I obey my Father's commandments and remain in his love." John 15:10

"For merely listening to the law doesn't make us right with God. It is obeying the law that makes us right in his sight." Romans 2:13

"Because one person disobeyed God, many became sinners. But because one other person obeyed God, many will be made righteous." Romans 5:19

"Don't just listen to God's word. You must do what it says. Otherwise, you are only fooling yourselves. For if you listen to the word and don't obey, it is like glancing at your face in a mirror. You see yourself, walk away, and forget what you look like. But if you look carefully into the perfect law that sets you free, and if you do what it says and don't forget what you heard, then God will bless you for doing it." James 1:22-25

"And this world is fading away, along with everything that people crave. But anyone who does what pleases God will live forever." 1 John 2:17

What does it mean to obey?

____

____

Is it important to be obedient? Why?

____

____

What helps us to obey Jesus?

____

____

Word Search

T	R	U	S	T	X	O	P	Y	B
E	B	Z	T	R	R	Q	Y	V	Z
W	I	B	L	E	S	S	I	N	G
O	B	T	C	O	M	M	A	N	D
R	L	J	P	R	O	T	E	C	T
D	E	U	F	P	G	V	R	H	R
O	D	D	C	A	V	J	K	K	E
B	E	L	I	E	V	E	F	J	L
E	T	L	I	S	T	E	N	L	Y
Y	X	E	M	G	D	R	K	Y	X

Blessing
Command
Obey
Believe
Listen
Word
Protect
Trust
Bible
Rely

Prayer

Prayer isn't complicated. It's simply talking to Jesus. Some people like to write prayers down in a journal. Some people say their prayers out loud. Some people like to save their prayers in a box.

King David wrote down many prayers. You can read them in the Psalms. David prayed when he was in trouble. He prayed when he was happy. He prayed when he was sad. He even prayed when he sinned! The Bible tells us to pray in all situations. God promises to answer as we pray according to His will.

Spend time praying AND listening. Prayer is a conversation with God. Allow Him to speak to your heart! When we pray and talk to Jesus, we are building a strong friendship with Him. Whether you are happy, sad, angry, discouraged, or in trouble talk to Jesus!

"May you hear the humble and earnest requests from me and your people Israel when we pray toward this place. Yes, hear us from heaven where you live, and when you hear, forgive."2 Chronicles 6:21

"The LORD has heard my plea; the LORD will answer my prayer." Psalm 6:9

"I am praying to you because I know you will answer, O God. Bend down and listen as I pray. Show me your unfailing love in wonderful ways. By your mighty power you rescue those who seek refuge from their enemies."
Psalm 17:6-7

"The LORD hears his people when they call to him for help. He rescues them from all their troubles." Psalm 34:17

"But I will call on God, and the LORD will rescue me. Morning, noon, and night I cry out in my distress, and the LORD hears my voice. He ransoms me and keeps me safe from the battle waged against me, though many still oppose me." Psalm 55:16-18

"When they call on me, I will answer; I will be with them in trouble. I will rescue and honor them." Psalm 91:15

"O LORD, I am calling to you. Please hurry! Listen when I cry to you for help! Accept my prayer as incense offered to you, and my upraised hands as an evening offering." Psalm 141:1-2

"I will answer them before they even call to me. While they are still talking about their needs, I will go ahead and answer their prayers!" Isaiah 65:24

"For I know the plans I have for you," says the LORD. "They are plans for good and not for disaster, to give you a future and a hope. In those days when you pray, I will listen." Jeremiah 29:11-12

"But when you pray, go away by yourself, shut the door behind you, and pray to your Father in private. Then your Father, who sees everything, will reward you." When you pray, don't babble on and on as the Gentiles do. They think their prayers are answered merely by repeating their words again and again. Don't be like them, for your Father knows exactly what you need even before you ask Him!" Matthew 6:6-7

"Keep on asking, and you will receive what you ask for. Keep on seeking, and you will find. Keep on knocking, and the door will be opened to you. For everyone who asks, receives. Everyone who seeks, finds. And to everyone who knocks, the door will be opened." Matthew 7:7-8

"But if you remain in me and my words remain in you, you may ask for anything you want, and it will be granted!" John 15:7

"Pray in the Spirit at all times and on every occasion. Stay alert and be persistent in your prayers for all believers everywhere." Ephesians 6:18

"Don't worry about anything; instead, pray about everything. Tell God what you need, and thank him for all he has done. Then you will experience God's peace, which exceeds anything we can understand. His peace will guard your hearts and minds as you live in Christ Jesus." Philippians 4:6-7

What does it mean to pray?

What is your favorite Scripture about prayer?

Praying is talking to God. Write out your prayer requests here.

Word Search

W H D N P R A Y I P
H E H E A L I N G V
A L F Q P W C L U X
N P B Z G P T G A G
S R E U G L R K B Q
W O L Z S U U N T M
E M I S V R S O S C
R I E S E Z T C A M
A S V H E E H K S P
P E E A X N K J K E

Believe	Promise	Answer	Pray
Knock	Trust	Healing	Help
Seek	Ask		

Promises from the Beatitudes

In life, you will face tough times even though you're following God! Jesus shared 9 special promises called the Beatitudes. The Beatitudes will help you when things get tough! (Read Matthew 5)

When we feel like we have nothing to give God, and see our need for Jesus, God promises us the Kingdom of Heaven! When we are sad and mourn, He promises to comfort us. When we are humble and think of others first, God promises us the whole earth! (Say what?!)

When we hunger for righteousness, He will fill us with himself! When we forgive others and show them mercy we will receive mercy! When our hearts are pure, we will see God at work all around us! When we work for peace among others, God will call us His Children as we spread His peace through the world.

When we are being made fun of because of our faith in Jesus, we can even rejoice because our reward is great. If you are going through a tough time, hold on to these precious promises from Jesus!

"God blesses those who are poor and realize their need for him, for the Kingdom of Heaven is theirs.

God blesses those who mourn, for they will be comforted.

God blesses those who are humble, for they will inherit the whole earth.

God blesses those who hunger and thirst for justice, for they will be satisfied.

God blesses those who are merciful, for they will be shown mercy.

God blesses those whose hearts are pure, for they will see God.

God blesses those who work for peace, for they will be called the children of God.

God blesses those who are persecuted for doing right, for the Kingdom of Heaven is theirs.

"God blesses you when people mock you and persecute you and lie about you and say all sorts of evil things against you because you are my followers. Be happy about it! Be very glad! For a great reward awaits you in heaven. And remember, the ancient prophets were persecuted in the same way." Matthew 5:3-12

What is your favorite Beatitude? Why?

How can the Beatitudes help us when we are going through a tough time?

What promises are you holding onto today?

Word Scramble

GOD ____________

LESBSES ____________

TSHEO ____________

HWEOS ____________

EASTHR ____________

ERA ____________

UEPR ____________

FRO ____________

TYEH ____________

LLIW ____________

ESE ____________

Answer key:
God blesses those whose hearts are pure, for they will see God.

Have you ever had a hard time sleeping? Many things can keep us from resting. But God promises to give us rest in Him!

Jesus said in Matthew 11:28, "Come to me, all of you who are weary and carry heavy burdens, and I will give you rest."

This rest is a special peace that will comfort you even when things are crazy. We can cast all our burdens and troubles on Jesus. He will help us in tough times and give us the rest we need.

Pray like this: "God, I need rest. Would you help me to give my cares to you so I can rest. Fill my bedroom with your Presence. In Jesus' name, amen!

"I lay down and slept, yet I woke up in safety, for the Lord was watching over me. I am not afraid of ten thousand enemies who surround me on every side." Psalms 3:5-6

"In peace I will lie down and sleep, for you alone, O Lord, will keep me safe." Psalms 4:8

"Give your burdens to the Lord, and he will take care of you. He will not permit the godly to slip and fall." Psalms 55:22

"Let my soul be at rest again, for the Lord has been good to me." Psalms 116:7

"You can go to bed without fear; you will lie down and sleep soundly. You need not be afraid of sudden disaster or the destruction that comes upon the wicked, for the Lord is your security. He will keep your foot from being caught in a trap." Proverbs 3:24-26

"You will keep in perfect peace all who trust in you, all whose thoughts are fixed on you!" Isaiah 26:3

"So don't worry about tomorrow, for tomorrow will bring its own worries. Today's trouble is enough for today." Matthew 6:34

"Then Jesus said, "Come to me, all of you who are weary and carry heavy burdens, and I will give you rest." Matthew 11:28

"Don't worry about anything; instead, pray about everything. Tell God what you need, and thank him for all he has done. Then you will experience God's peace, which exceeds anything we can understand. His peace will guard your hearts and minds as you live in Christ Jesus." Philippians 4:6-7

"Give all your worries and cares to God, for he cares about you." 1 Peter 5:7

What can we do if we are having trouble sleeping?

What Scripture can help you rest and sleep?

Share about a time God helped you rest.

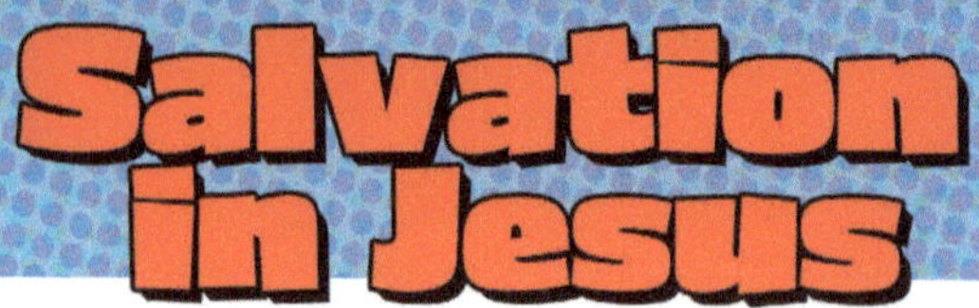

The Bible tells us that God created everything in the universe. God created the first man and woman - Adam and Eve. Adam and Eve sinned by listening to Satan and eating the fruit from the tree of the Knowledge of Good and Evil. (Read Genesis 3). Because they disobeyed God, sin infected the entire human race.

We all sin and our sin separates us from God. The Bible tells us sin results in death. But God made a way for us to overcome sin! He sent His Son Jesus to become a man, suffer and die for our sins on a cross. By faith in Jesus, you can be free from sin!

Now we can be reunited with God and he part of His family forever! But first, we must respond to God's invitation.

How can you begin a new life with Jesus Christ? It's as easy as A-B-C!

Admit you have sinned.

Believe Jesus died for your sins.

Confess that Jesus is your Lord and Savior!

Pray like this: "Jesus, I know I have sinned. I believe you died and took the place for my punishment. I ask you to come into my heart and be my Lord and Savior!"

"For a child is born to us, a son is given to us. The government will rest on his shoulders. And He will be called: Wonderful Counselor, Mighty God, Everlasting Father, Prince of Peace." Isaiah 9:6

"Yet it was our weaknesses he carried; it was our sorrows that weighed him down. And we thought his troubles were a punishment from God, a punishment for his own sins! But he was pierced for our rebellion, crushed for our sins. He was beaten so we could be whole. He was whipped so we could be healed. All of us, like sheep, have strayed away. We have left God's paths to follow our own. Yet the LORD laid on him the sins of us all." Isaiah 53:4-6

"In those days and at that time I will raise up a righteous descendant from King David's line. He will do what is just and right throughout the land. In that day Judah will be saved, and Jerusalem will live in safety. And this will be its name: 'The LORD Is Our Righteousness.' For this is what the LORD says: David will have a descendant sitting on the throne of Israel forever"Jeremiah 33:15-17

"I baptize with water those who repent of their sins and turn to God. But someone is coming soon who is greater than I am—so much greater that I'm not worthy even to be his slave and carry his sandals. He will baptize you with the Holy Spirit and with fire." Matthew 3:11

"But to all who believed him and accepted him, he gave the right to become children of God. They are reborn—not with a physical birth resulting from human passion or plan, but a birth that comes from God." John 1:12-13

"Look! The Lamb of God who takes away the sin of the world!" John 1:29

"For this is how God loved the world: He gave his one and only Son, so that everyone who believes in him will not perish but have eternal life. God sent his Son into the world not to judge the world, but to save the world through him." John 3:16-17

"For the sin of this one man, Adam, caused death to rule over many. But even greater is God's wonderful grace and his gift of righteousness, for all who receive it will live in triumph over sin and death through this one man, Jesus Christ." Romans 5:17

"If you confess with your mouth that Jesus is Lord and believe in your heart that God raised him from the dead, you will be saved." Romans 10:9

"Anyone who belongs to Christ has become a new person. The old life is gone; a new life has begun!" 2 Corinthians 5:17

"For God made Christ, who never sinned, to be the offering for our sin, so that we could be made right with God through Christ." 2 Corinthians 5:21

"You were dead because of your sins and because your sinful nature was not yet cut away. Then God made you alive with Christ, for he forgave all our sins. He canceled the record of the charges against us and took it away by nailing it to the cross." Colossians 2:13-14

"This is a trustworthy saying, and everyone should accept it: "Christ Jesus came into the world to save sinners"—and I am the worst of them all." 1 Timothy 1:15

What did Jesus do for us to be saved?

____

____

How can you be saved?

____

____

Did you pray to accept Jesus? Write your prayer and the date here.

____

____

____

____

Word Scramble

NSFOCSE ______

TIWH ______

OURY ______

MOTHU ______

NAD ______

BEIVEEL ______

NI ______

TRHAE ______

UYO ______

LSALH ______

EB ______

DASEV ______

Answer Key:
Confess with your mouth and believe in your heart, you shall be saved.

What we say matters. Life and death are in the power of the tongue. Our tongue is the hardest thing to tame. We can train dogs and even elephants, but often we can't control what we say. We can bless God with our speech, and then we can turn around and yell all kinds of mean things to our family and friends.

It is important to read Scriptures about our speech because if we can control our words, we can control ourselves. Jesus wants to help us master our speech so that we can speak things that are good and life giving to bless others. He does not want us to speak harm to our friends, family, and those around us.

"May the words of my mouth and the meditation of my heart be pleasing to you, O Lord, my rock and my redeemer." Psalm 19:14

"Keep your tongue from speaking evil and your lips from telling lies! Turn away from evil and do good. Search for peace, and work to maintain it." Psalm 34:12-14

"A gossip goes around telling secrets, but those who are trustworthy can keep a confidence." Proverbs 11:13

"A troublemaker plants seeds of strife; gossip separates the best of friends." Proverbs 16:28

"Rumors are dainty morsels that sink deep into one's heart." Proverbs 18:8

"The tongue can bring death or life; those who love to talk will reap the consequences." Proverbs 18:21

"A gossip goes around telling secrets, so don't hang around with chatterers." Proverbs 20:19

"As surely as a north wind brings rain, so a gossiping tongue causes anger!" Proverbs 25:23

"Fire goes out without wood, and quarrels disappear when gossip stops." Proverbs 26:20

"Don't use foul or abusive language. Let everything you say be good and helpful, so that your words will be an encouragement to those who hear them." Ephesians 4:29

Why are our words important?

____

____

Which body part is the hardest to tame? Why?

____

____

How can we change our speech?

____

____

Word of God

Life often brings tough times. Just as David faced the giant Goliath, you will face many giants in this life. Their names are fear, temptation, pride, loneliness, and many others. But like David, you have a weapon against the giants of life - The Living Word of God! The Word of God is like a weapon in your hands against these giants.

Satan tried tempting Jesus when he started His ministry. Satan tempted him with food after Jesus ate nothing for 40 days. He tempted Jesus to jump off a tower so angels could catch Him. And lastly, Satan tempted Jesus with power if Jesus would worship him instead of God. Each time, Jesus fought Satan with the Word of God! (Luke 4:1-13)

"For the word of God is alive and powerful. It is sharper than the sharpest two-edged sword, cutting between soul and spirit, between joint and marrow. It exposes our innermost thoughts and desires." Hebrews 4:12

When you face tough times, grab your weapon - The Living Word of God!

"So commit yourselves wholeheartedly to these words of mine. Tie them to your hands and wear them on your forehead as reminders. Teach them to your children. Talk about them when you are at home and when you are on the road, when you are going to bed and when you are getting up. Write them on the doorposts of your house and on your gates." Deuteronomy 11:18-20

"Study this Book of Instruction continually. Meditate on it day and night so you will be sure to obey everything written in it. Only then will you prosper and succeed in all you do." Joshua 1:8

"Joyful are people of integrity, who follow the instructions of the LORD. Joyful are those who obey his laws and search for Him with all their hearts."
Psalm 119:1-2

"How can a young person stay pure? By obeying your Word." Psalm 119:9

"Make me walk along the path of your commands, for that is where my happiness is found."Psalm 119:35

"Your word is a lamp to guide my feet and a light for my path." Psalm 119:105

"Anyone who listens to my teaching and follows it is wise, like a person who builds a house on solid rock. Though the rain comes in torrents and the floodwaters rise and the winds beat against that house, it won't collapse because it is built on bedrock. But anyone who hears my teaching and doesn't obey it is foolish, like a person who builds a house on sand. When the rains and floods come and the winds beat against that house, it will collapse with a mighty crash." Matthew 7:24-27

"For the word of God will never fail." Luke 1:37

In the beginning the Word already existed. The Word was with God, and the Word was God. He existed in the beginning with God. God created everything through him, and nothing was created except through him. The Word gave life to everything that was created, and his life brought light to everyone. The light shines in the darkness, and the darkness can never extinguish it." John 1:1-5

"And now I entrust you to God and the message of his grace that is able to build you up and give you an inheritance with all those he has set apart for himself." Acts 20:32

"All Scripture is inspired by God and is useful to teach us what is true and to make us realize what is wrong in our lives. It corrects us when we are wrong and teaches us to do what is right. God uses it to prepare and equip his people to do every good work." 2 Timothy 3:16-17

"For the word of God is alive and powerful. It is sharper than the sharpest two-edged sword, cutting between soul and spirit, between joint and marrow. It exposes our innermost thoughts and desires." Hebrews 4:12

"But don't just listen to God's word. You must do what it says. Otherwise, you are only fooling yourselves. For if you listen to the word and don't obey, it is like glancing at your face in a mirror. You see yourself, walk away, and forget what you look like. But if you look carefully into the perfect law that sets you free, and if you do what it says and don't forget what you heard, then God will bless you for doing it." James 1:22-25

"For you have been born again, but not to a life that will quickly end. Your new life will last forever because it comes from the eternal, living word of God." 1 Peter 1:23

Why is the Bible important?

____

____

How does God speak to us through the Bible?

____

____

What is your favorite Scripture? Why?

____

____

Q	H	P	W	V	S	E	Z	B	S
B	S	E	R	J	Y	D	G	L	W
X	P	A	L	O	E	V	O	A	O
B	T	L	L	P	M	S	D	M	R
H	I	A	I	V	Q	I	U	P	D
O	F	B	N	G	A	V	S	S	I
L	D	E	L	F	H	T	Q	E	Y
Y	Z	U	V	E	O	T	I	F	O
A	X	K	M	U	O	L	J	O	Q
R	C	M	H	O	J	S	L	Z	N

Salvation	Promise	Jesus	Bible
Sword	Light	Holy	Help
Lamp	GOD		

The Bible tells us that God inhabits the praises of His people. When we spend time worshiping Jesus He promises to show up as we worship!

Praise and Worship involves your mouth, body, and heart. It can be through a song, a prayer, and even how we act towards others. Your worship is special to God. After all, you were created to worship and live in relationship with Him!

You can meet with God through worship anywhere: in your backyard, at school, in your car or at church!

Spend some time worshiping Jesus now!

"The LORD is my strength and my song; he has given me victory. This is my God, and I will praise him—my father's God, and I will exalt him!" Exodus 15:2

"Give to the LORD the glory he deserves! Bring your offering and come into his presence. Worship the LORD in all his holy splendor." 1 Chronicles 16:29

"I will thank the LORD because He is just; I will sing praise to the name of the LORD Most High."
Psalm 7:17

"Honor the LORD, you heavenly beings; honor the LORD for his glory and strength. Honor the LORD for the glory of his name. Worship the LORD in the splendor of his holiness." Psalm 29:1-2

"Shout joyful praises to God, all the earth! Sing about the glory of his name! Tell the world how glorious he is. Say to God, "How awesome are your deeds! Your enemies cringe before your mighty power. Everything on earth will worship you; they will sing your praises, shouting your name in glorious songs." Psalm 66:1-4

"We thank you, O God! We give thanks because you are near. People everywhere tell of your wonderful deeds." Psalm 75:1

"All the nations you made will come and bow before you, Lord; they will praise your holy name. For you are great and perform wonderful deeds. You alone are God." Psalm 86:9-10

Come, let us sing to the LORD! Let us shout joyfully to the Rock of our salvation. Let us come to him with thanksgiving. Let us sing psalms of praise to him. For the LORD is a great God, a great King above all gods. He holds in his hands the depths of the earth and the mightiest mountains. The sea belongs to him, for He made it. His hands formed the dry land, too. Come, let us worship and bow down. Let us kneel before the LORD our maker, for he is our God. We are the people he watches over, the flock under his care." Psalm 95:1-7

"Exalt the LORD our God, and worship at his holy mountain in Jerusalem, for the LORD our God is holy!" Psalm 99:9

"Shout with joy to the LORD, all the earth! Worship the LORD with gladness. Come before him, singing with joy. Acknowledge that the LORD is God! He made us, and we are his. We are his people, the sheep of his pasture.

Enter his gates with thanksgiving; go into his courts with praise. Give thanks to him and praise his name. For the LORD is good. His unfailing love continues forever, and his faithfulness continues to each generation." Psalm 100

"Sing to the LORD! Praise the LORD! For though I was poor and needy, he rescued me from my oppressors." Jeremiah 20:13

"But the time is coming—indeed it's here now—when true worshipers will worship the Father in spirit and in truth. The Father is looking for those who will worship him that way. For God is Spirit, so those who worship him must worship in spirit and in truth." John 4:23-24

"And so, dear brothers and sisters, I plead with you to give your bodies to God because of all he has done for you. Let them be a living and holy sacrifice—the kind he will find acceptable. This is truly the way to worship him. Don't copy the behavior and customs of this world, but let God transform you into a new person by changing the way you think. Then you will learn to know God's will for you, which is good and pleasing and perfect." Romans 12:1-2

What are different ways to worship God?

How can you worship God with your heart?

When we worship, God promises to draw near. Share about a time when you spent time in God's presence.

Word Scramble

IHPWOSR

GDO

NI

RITSIP

DAN

NI

RTUTH

Answer key:
Worship God in Spirit and in Truth!

How to use for Small Groups

1. Select the topics you would like to cover during your group's time frame. (If you will meet for 10 weeks, choose 10 topics, etc.) Select 3-5 Scriptures to read during the study. Print out take home pages of the full Scriptures and games from the website.

2. To prepare for the group, pray for the children prior to your study with that week's topic in mind. Print out the provided take home pages and game pages.

3. Start the study by reading the introduction. Then, have the children take turns reading the Scriptures. Discuss and answer the questions as a group. Allow the children time to complete the game page. Send each child home with a topic review page.

To print hand outs and games, visit

The-Olive-Press.com/prints

Do all the kids in your group have a Bible?
If they don't, we recommend the
New Living Translation.
This version is great for young readers!

This book is intended for readers ages 5-12.
For children ages 0-4, please see
The Little Book of Bible Promises.
All books are available for purchase at
The-Olive-Press.com

As you read through these Scriptures, remember that these are just selections from a big Bible filled with all sorts of promises. We may not understand it all, but the Holy Spirit is our teacher and guide. Jesus gives us the ability to understand and live out the promises He has given us through His Word.

It is our prayer that you take hold of the Word of God, and stand firm on God's promises for your life. For in the beginning was the Word. The Word was with God and The Word *was* God (See John 1:1). The Word is alive, active, and sharper than any two edged sword (see Hebrews 4:12). The Word is also God-breathed and still applicable today (see 2 Timothy 3:16).

Remember that Jesus is with you, even until the end of time. And He will be with you for all of eternity!

www.ingramcontent.com/pod-product-compliance
Ingram Content Group UK Ltd.
Pitfield, Milton Keynes, MK11 3LW, UK
UKHW062255290726
14090UKWH00017B/695